Old Udny, Tarves and Methlick

by Donna M. Donald

On the right of this view of Duthie Road in Tarves is the Bank building, once home to Aberdeen Town and County Bank. A little further along (not seen in this view) is the school, still in operation, dating from 1911. On the left, there was once a variety of shops, including Cummings bakery, which was first opened in 1858. A family-run firm, the shop finally closed only a few years ago.

Text © Donna M. Donald, 2007
First published in the United Kingdom, 2007,
by Stenlake Publishing Ltd.
www.stenlake.co.uk
ISBN 9781840334005

Further Reading

The books listed below were used by the author during her research. Only *Old Ellon* is available from Stenlake Publishing; for the rest please contact your local bookshop or reference library.

Abel, George, *Wylins Fae My Wallet* (Alex. Gardner, Paisley, 1916).
Argo, Mrs M. A., *Annals of Udny: A History of Udny from Early Times to the Middle of the Nineteenth Century* (George Deans, 1926).
Birnie, Linda, *Old Ellon* (Stenlake Publishing, 2005).
Cairnorrie WRI, *The Book of Methlick* (Aberdeen Journals, 1939).
Haddow, Angus H., *The History of Methlick Parish Church* (1997).
Johnston, William G., *Croft and Farms of Udny* (Famedram Publishers, 1998).
Porter, William A., *Tarves Lang Syne* (Maxiprint, 1996).
Pratt, J. B., *The Life and Death of Jamie Fleeman, the Laird of Udny's Fool* (first published 1831; Heritage Press, 1980).
Robertson, Margaret C., *Udny Green Church: A Short History and Guide* (1987).
Tarves Gaitherins, Volume 1 (Tarves Heritage Centre, 1991).
Toulmin, David, *The Tillycorthie Story* (Centre for Scottish Studies, University of Aberdeen, 1986).

Acknowledgements

Thanks to the people I met in the villages of Tarves and Methlick for all their invaluable help; the people at the Tarves Heritage Centre, an excellent resource centre with very helpful volunteers; my family for memories and stories; and Linda Birnie for advice and encouragement.

The War Memorial in Udny Green remembers 60 young men of the parish who gave their lives for King and Country in the First World War. The men served in various regiments, including the Gordon Highlanders, the Seaforths, the Machine Gun Core, the Highland Light Artillery and several more. One family, the Argos of Denend farm, lost two sons; their names are inscribed upon the memorial, and a family gravestone in Udny churchyard also commemorates them. One could say that the war was a great leveller, in the sense that both gentlemen and their servants were killed for the same cause. On the memorial is the name of Edmund Noble, son of the laird of Udny's gamekeeper, while inside the church is a marble tablet dedicated to the memory of Lieutenant Richard Udny, the laird's nephew, who was killed in action at the age of eighteen.

Udny

INTRODUCTION

'Whatever lands lie between the Rivers Ythan and Don one hears called by the name of Formartine among the inhabitants, who disdain to consider themselves as belonging to Buchan.' So said Sir William Forbes of Foveran in the seventeenth century, suggesting that the people of this part of what we now call Aberdeenshire were rather proud of their individuality and were not reticent about declaring it.

Udny, Tarves and Methlick lie in the north central area of Formartine, with Methlick's most distant edge being around 25 miles north-west of Aberdeen. These rural parishes were for centuries centres of agriculture. Now, however, their villages have become dormitory towns for those who commute daily to Aberdeen.

Once the area was served with a railway link to Aberdeen and beyond in the south, and Ellon, Peterhead and Fraserburgh in the north, with stations at Udny Station and Logierieve, also in the parish of Udny, but now commuters must rely on their cars or the bus. Few of the villages today have more than a single convenience store, whereas they once boasted butcher, baker and ironmonger, when they were truly the centre of the farming communities they served.

Five or six hundred years ago, the parishes we know today would be completely unrecognisable. Devoid of woodland, the area was mossy, stony, wet and uncompromising. The political machinations which affected Scotland's early history barely affected the people trying to scratch a living from the land. The first reference to the name Udny dates from November 1406, when Ranald de Uldney granted certain lands to the chaplain serving at the Chapel of the Holy Trinity (at Udny Green) for the soul of his father, Patrick. Other early spellings include Oudeni and Woodney. It is believed that this family had the barony from the beginning of the thirteenth century. The parish which is recognised today as Udny was formally created in 1597 from parts of Logie Buchan, Ellon, Tarves and Foveran parishes. The villages of Cultercullen, Udny Station, Udny Green and Pitmedden all come within Udny Parish, and on the western edge of the parish lies Whiterashes, a small settlement on the main A947 between Newmachar and Oldmeldrum.

The name of Tarves, according to the nineteenth-century schoolmaster David Milne of King Edward, stands for an inn or place of hospitality on a height, from the Gaelic *tor* (height) and *uis* (hospitality or comfort). It was certainly situated on a hill, and the land round about was stony and bare, not particularly hospitable for early dwellers, but rich enough for the area to be presented by William the Lion to the Abbot of Arbroath Abbey when it was founded in 1176. It was a key settlement on the drove road between Aikey Fair, near Old Deer, and the Falkirk Tryst. There was a 'commonty', or common land, for resting the cattle at Raxton Howe, a little way south of the Tangland ford where the cattle crossed the Ythan. In Tarves parish lie the settlements of Barthol Chapel and Craigdam, and the seat of Schivas as well as Tolquhon Castle and Haddo House.

The name Methlick – spelled Methlayk – appears first in the fourteenth century, when the parish was split into two halves: the sunny half and the shadow half. In the fifteenth century, James Gordon of Haldauch (Haddo) married Canea Harper, heiress to the sunny half of Methlick, thus adding these lands to his estate. He later acquired the shadow half of Methlick, apart from 'le Chrystis Croft', and thus the parish as we know it today was reunited under one landowner. Also within Methlick parish is the hamlet of Cairnorrie, which until very recently had its own tiny primary school.

Finds of arrowheads and urns on farms indicate that early man inhabited this area. In early times, the Church was well represented, with farm names such as Andet, Chapelpark, Cloisterseat and Orchardtown indicating sites of religious settlements. There is no mention of these names, however, in the Book of Deer, the document produced by the Cistercian monks of Deer Abbey. Nonetheless, St Ninian, following in the tracks of Roman legions in the Methlick area in the fifth century, founded a church at Andet, a name which means 'mother church of a district'. Moreover, on ground between Little Water and Overton of Ardo, a well was named for St Devenick, the patron saint of Methlick, the water from which was believed to facilitate miraculous cures. Tokens of thanks, rags tied on the nearby bushes, were left by those seeking a miracle. Udny Green boasted a Chapel of the Holy Trinity, an emblem of the power of the church, and then in 1604 'Christ's Kirk' was built at the Green, albeit one of 'plain design and thatched with heather'. Pitmedden is said to have been named for St Medan, with a chapel and graveyard of that name situated nearby.

Family names of those occupying the great houses and castles, according to documentary evidence of the fifteenth and sixteenth centuries, include Panton at Pitmedden, Udny at Udny Castle, the Gordons at Haddo, Forbes at Tolquhon and Schevez at Schivas. Amazingly, the Gordons remain at Haddo, now a National Trust for Scotland property, while an Udny lived at the castle near Udny Green until the 1930s. Schivas is currently in private hands; Pitmedden, famous now for its formal, walled garden, is also in the hands of the NTS. Tolquhon, long since sold by the Forbes family, is in a ruinous state, having fallen into disrepair after being left vacant from the mid-nineteenth century.

Much of the lands of Tarves and Methlick was owned by the Gordons of Haddo, and this family also owned property in the parish of Udny. The Udny family had land elsewhere in Aberdeenshire, notably in the Foveran and Newburgh areas, as well as their seat at Udny Green. The Setons, who acquired Pitmedden and other lands of the present-day parish from the Panton family, retained their estate until the end of the nineteenth century, owning also the estates of Dumbreck, Orchardtown and Logierieve from the mid-seventeenth to mid-eighteenth centuries.

The rural communities of Udny, Tarves and Methlick are no longer in the control of the feudal landowners as they once were, many of the farms and crofts now being in private ownership. For administrative purposes, Gordon District (in which all three parishes lie) has its headquarters in Inverurie, while for employment many make the journey into Aberdeen daily. Secondary schooling is provided at Oldmeldrum and Ellon. Local GPs hold surgeries in each of the villages, but hospital services, once provided by a cottage hospital in Tarves, are now only available in Aberdeen.

Udny Station did not become a village in its own right until the latter half of the nineteenth century with the advent of the railway, as the name suggests. The big farm estates around Udny Station – Tillery, Tillycorthie, Fiddes, Monkshill, Orchardtown, Tillygrieg – all feature in the history books, and clearly from their names, some would once have had important religious significance for the area. Cultercullen, a smaller settlement further along the road towards Foveran, was the location of the school. But just as villages grew up over the years at fords in rivers and at key crossroads, villages in the north-east expanded rapidly with the opening of the Formartine and Buchan Railway. Thus it was with the small hamlet where the Great North of Scotland Railway built the first station in the parish of Udny. Suddenly, commuters required a bank (seen to the left), a hotel (on the right) and additional housing. From 1904 to 1907, the Great North of Scotland Railway ran an omnibus service from Methlick through Tarves and Haddo to Udny Station to meet the trains to and from Aberdeen, Ellon, Peterhead and Fraserburgh, allowing people from these rural parishes easy access to the world beyond their immediate doorstep, and making Udny Station a bustling village.

In the 1960s, the last passenger trains ran from Aberdeen on the Buchan and Formartine line. By then, people were commuting by car and bus, and the railways were in decline. The final goods train ran through Udny Station in 1979, after which the railway was torn up and eventually became a walkway. Even before closure of the line, the station building on the platform was demolished to make way for housing. Following closure, the goods yard was made into a playpark. The lengthy platform can still be seen today, and there are the remains of a signal box a little way out of the village.

This general merchant's shop at the junction of the main Aberdeen–Tarves road and the Udny Station turn-off served the community for many years, finally closing in the late 1970s. Shops in rural locations – outside a village – were common in the days when people walked or cycled everywhere. As the popularity of the motor car grew, grocers', bakers' and butchers' vans became regular sights on the roads, as many people living in the country on farms and crofts as tenants or workers could not afford a motor car. Farmers' or farm workers' wives would swap a dozen eggs from the hens and ducks they kept for groceries from the van, and thus the grocer had fine fresh eggs to take to his village customers.

Tillycorthie, meaning the site of a standing stone ('Corthie') would at one time have been the site of a stone circle or perhaps even a castle. No trace of these remain; however, there is a twentieth-century version of a castle at Tillycorthie, which in 1912 was one of the first reinforced concrete buildings to be constructed in Scotland. It was built by tin-mining entrepreneur, James Duncan, a man who came from humble beginnings in New Leeds in Buchan, to make his fortune in Bolivia, and spend his latter years living in luxury in Udny. The total of Duncan's estate in Udny extended to some 526 acres, and he owned farms at Ellon and Longside as well. Incorporated into the design of the house were many features of a Spanish villa, no doubt inspired by Duncan's travels in South America, and inside there were murals, friezes, panelled rooms, a walk-in strong-room safe and, most unusually, a urinal instead of a lavatory in one of the bathrooms! Duncan brought up a family of eight in this home and when he died in 1938, his widow continued to run the estate until her death in 1953. The University of Aberdeen bought the estate, using the mansion house as a store. It was subsequently sold and developed, and was split into flats. The lodges and 'cottar' houses on the estate were also all sold to private individuals, although the university continued to farm some of the land.

James Duncan of Tillycorthie is remembered as something of an eccentric – for instance, his grandchildren remember him placing chestnuts on the fire so that they exploded onto the carpet to entertain his young visitors – but he is also remembered in the village of Udny Station in the form of bricks and mortar. In addition to providing the village with a hall, built in 1915, now a store, he built flats to house his estate workers. These houses, of local and Stirlinghill granite, form Woodside Terrace. Across the road a row of houses was built some time later and named Duncan Terrace in his memory. One of the houses in Duncan Terrace was built by Duncan for his eldest daughter and her husband, and named after the ship on which they met, the *Orcoma*, travelling across the Atlantic to South America. Duncan also brought electric lighting to Udny Station, thanks to the Duncan Electricity Company, which also served Kintore, Ellon and Ballater.

Tillery estate lies a little to the south of Udny Station and Tillycorthie. In the 1930s it was home to W. K. A. J. Chambers-Hunter, who was a supporter of Oswald Mosley and his British Union of Fascists political party, known as the 'Blackshirts'. Mosley was a supporter of Mussolini, meeting him in Italy in 1932, and he was married in Goebbels' drawing room with Adolf Hitler in attendance in 1936. It is said that during this time, Chambers-Hunter, author of a publication entitled *British Union and Social Credit*, was so delighted to welcome Mosley on a visit to Tillery that he placed a large sign adorned with the black lightning symbol of Mosley's party in the field at the junction of the Tillery and Aberdeen roads. Some local workers, in opposition to the policies of the Blackshirts, knocked the sign down. Chambers-Hunter reinstated it. Again it was knocked over. Furious, and determined that this would not happen again, Chambers-Hunter attached a sign to the chassis of a lorry … and then buried the lorry in his field. For years, Tillery hosted games – an annual event which attracted people from far and wide. These games were held even after the big house burned down some time before the Second World War.

The area known as Logierieve lies at the eastern edge of the parish of Udny and was once the site of an extensive peat moss, reflected in the names of local farms and crofts such as 'Mosstown'. The name derives from Gaelic, meaning 'a hollow enclosure for animals', and it continues to be a centre for agriculture, being the location of a farm contracting business and, until the 1980s, a blacksmith's business. The railway ran through Logierieve and there was a station there, the final stop before Ellon. The platform and station house complete with station clock, although no longer working, are still in existence and can be seen from the Formartine and Buchan walkway. According to records, along with nearby Orchardtown, Logierieve formed part of the ancient barony of Tulliedaff, owned by a family of the same name. In the seventeenth century, the estate was owned by the Setons of Pitmedden, and when their estate was being broken up in the early part of the eighteenth century, Logierieve and other parts were bought by the Governors of Gordon's Hospital, which later became Aberdeen Endowments Trust. The estate of Logierieve was then rented to a family named Legertwood for 999 years, who built Logierieve House (seen here) in the mid-nineteenth century. The family continued to live in the house until early in the twentieth century, when they gave up the estate.

The Mill of Udny, between the Home Farm of Udny estate and the main road to Aberdeen, was fed by the Bronie Burn. In 1800, it was one of ten working mills in Udny. Built in the middle of the eighteenth century by a forward-thinking laird, it remained in operation until the 1920s. In 1867, a most generous miller by the name of Jamieson left in his will the residue of his estate to the Kirk Session of Udny Green for the benefit 'of the aged and infirm of the parish'. However, once the few bequests he had made were paid, very little remained of his estate. At the sale of his effects, a local man purchased Jamieson's old kist, took it home and came upon a pleasant surprise – £1,100 was hidden in a secret drawer. The honest parishioner handed the money over to the Kirk Session and was rewarded with £5 and the interest on £100 for life.

Udny Post Office and General Merchants is situated on the old road a little way from Pitmedden at the junction of the Aberdeen and Logierieve roads. Owned at the beginning of the twentieth century by A. W. Giles, the shop was known locally as 'Tolly Giles' or 'Tollies'. No documentary evidence exists but belief has it that this was once the location of a toll house, and being at a junction this is certainly likely. After A. W. Giles retired, the post office and shop was run by two generations of the Johnston family for around 70 years, and it remains Udny's only post office. Across the road from the post office, lying a little way up the hill towards the Mill of Allathan where there was a gravel quarry for many years, is the house known as Housieside. It and its neighbouring house were demolished some time before the 1930s, when the present two houses – Maplebank and The Bungalow – were built. The latter house was built for the retiring gamekeeper of Udny Estate, John Noble, to his own design. The author's father, a grandson of John Noble, continues to live in that house to the present day.

The Six Gates, roughly halfway between Udny Green and the post office, lie in a hollow and are reputedly haunted by a ghostly Green Lady. The six gates barred the entrances to four fields, a track which leads up to Udny Castle and another down to the estate's Keeper's Cottage, beyond which runs the Bronie Burn.

The South Lodge of Udny Castle. The Udny motto, 'All my trust is in God', is fitting, given the long association of the family with the Church, first documented when the laird granted lands to the chaplain serving in Udny Green's Church of the Holy Trinity in 1406. However, the Udnys also put their faith in solid stone when building the tower of Udny Castle in the early fourteenth century. Unfortunately its thick walls and sturdy doors were not enough to keep out the Covenanters, who raided the Castle in protest at the Udny family's strong anti-Covenanting beliefs. The original tower keep was increased in height by an extra storey and in the nineteenth century large wings were added. They were demolished in the 1960s. The castle is situated east of Udny Green, and lodges stand at the entrances to the policies at the Green and at the northern side on the Pitmedden–Oldmeldrum road.

The Victorian additions to Udny Castle can be seen in this view. In the seventeenth century the Udnys also owned lands at Belhelvie and Newburgh, and the castle at Knockhall in the Newburgh estate, which the family used as their seat for some years. Knockhall is associated with Jamie Fleeman, the Laird of Udny's fool and perhaps Udny's most famous resident. Born at Ludquarn, Longside in 1713, Fleeman once saved the Udny family's charter chest from a fire that engulfed Knockhall Castle. He was alerted to the blaze by one of the castle's dogs, told the gardener to evacuate the castle, then returned to the charter room himself. Lifting the 4 foot by 4 foot iron-plated chest – which normally required three men to lift it – he threw it out of the window to safety below. For this bravery, the Laird of Udny allowed him a peck of meal and sixpence a week for life. He also received a shoe allowance, but rarely availed himself of that luxury. Fleeman died in 1778 and was buried in his home parish of Longside. He is remembered fondly in Udny, not least for his cutting retort to a question posed by a gentleman of some status: 'I'm Udny's feel. Fa's feel are ye?' ('I'm the Lord of Udny's fool. Whose fool are you?') In 1934 the last of the Udnys died and the estate was inherited by Lord Belhaven and Stenton, whose daughter now lives in the castle and runs Udny estate. Once the site of a fair held upon the third Tuesday in September which continued for three days, the castle grounds were also the location for the Formartine Agricultural Association's annual show in the late nineteenth century, and in more recent years, staged the Udny Games.

The present church building at Udny Green dates from 1821, replacing a much older church, known as Christ's Kirk, which had been situated in the churchyard. The clock in the tower was gifted in 1895 by Mrs Amy Udny, and after her death, her husband, the last Udny laird, had a stained glass window installed in her memory. Inside the church there is a marble table to the memory of this last laird installed by Lord Belhaven and Stenton, who inherited Udny estate in 1934. Four years later Lord Belhaven and his wife presented the church with a baptismal font for the baptism of their daughter Margaret. A long-serving minister of the parish, Dr Alexander Spence, is remembered in Udny by a communion table dedicated by his congregation after his death in 1923. He had served as minister for almost 50 years, and a second memorial to him, a new village hall called the Spence Memorial Hall, was built in 1937. In 1931 Udny Green Church and the United Free Church in Pitmedden were combined, with the Rev. William McNutt becoming the first minister to preach in both churches.

The churchyard at Udny Green, which serves the whole parish, contains the remains of the old 'Christ's Kirk', which in turn had replaced the Chapel of the Holy Trinity in 1604. Christ's Kirk was of 'plain design' and thatched with heather. It was partly rebuilt in 1760 and repaired in 1786, before finally being deemed too small for the parish and replaced in 1821. The actual site of this old church is around the vaults of the Setons of Pitmedden and the Pittrichie family. Many of the old gravestones tell stories about times long gone in far more thought-provoking ways than any history book could do. One such stone highlights the dreadful heartache of the Marr family of Coullie, who buried eight children in 1862 during a diphtheria outbreak. Another tells of a family tragedy: the son and heir of the Tillycorthie estate drowning in the Thames at the age of 23. In the churchyard there is a Roundhouse, dating from the 1830s, when the threat of body-snatching was at its height. The building has thick walls and a door of studded oak, and was designed to house a body for up to three months – by which time decomposition was such that the corpse would have been worthless to body-snatchers. The building cost £80 to construct and those who subscribed to building costs were permitted to use the facility for free. Others paid a fee to keep their loved ones from harm. By the time the Roundhouse was completed, body-snatching had become less prevalent and the building was rarely used for the purpose for which it had been intended. Thanks to its strength and solidity, it was later used as an ammunition store.

Udny Green's appearance, particularly round the green itself, has changed little over the centuries. Behind the row of houses on the south side of the green is the manse. Beside it there had once been a wayside inn, which in 1860 became the girls' school. The hall pictured was replaced in 1937 by the Spence Memorial Hall, built by the people of Udny in memory of their long-serving minister. To the right of the hall, the hotel was originally a farmhouse, owned by the Davidson family. Beside it is the entrance to the churchyard and at the other side of that was the site of Udny Academy, an establishment that prepared gentlemen's sons for university. Built in 1786, its catchment area included Tarves and Methlick. There were between 30 and 40 scholars at any one time, some of whom were boarders. In 1812 the house alongside the present church on the north side of the green was acquired to provide additional accommodation for the scholars. Udny Green continued to be a place of erudition into the twentieth century, with the Udny Public Library being founded in 1912 in a building also on the north side of the green, thanks to the generosity of David Walker of Coullie.

Pitmedden House. The origin of the name Pitmedden is a matter for debate: it could be Gaelic, meaning the middle (*meadhon*) place (*pit*), or it may be named for Saint Medan or Meddan, who founded a chapel at Dumbreck, a little way from the village. Whatever its etymology, Pitmedden is first mentioned in the history books as the estate of the Panton family, some time in the fourteenth century. The Pantons owned lands in the south of the present-day parish, at The Craig and Tillymaud. In 1603 the estate was acquired by John Seton, a staunch royalist, who fought against the Covenanters and lost his life at the Battle of the Brig o' Dee in 1639. His son, Alexander, opposed the re-establishment of Roman Catholicism and was forced to give up public office, including his post as Senator of the College of Justice. This, however, gave him the chance to plan and found the Great Garden of Pitmedden in 1675. It is said to have been inspired by the gardens at Vaux-le-Vicomte near Paris, which were designed for Louis XIV's finance minister by the man who later designed the gardens at the Palace of Versailles. The last Seton laird was Sir William Seton, who was responsible for building the existing Victorian house (seen here) in 1860. The house in which he was born was very badly damaged in 1818, the year of his birth, and it was eventually demolished to make way for the new building. In 1894 the estate was sold to Alexander Keith. He and his son, Major James Keith, improved their land by planting many trees and developing farming methods on estate farms. They also used the property's walled garden as a kitchen garden. After 1952, when Major James Keith signed the property over to the National Trust for Scotland, experts set about restoring the formal garden to its original seventeenth-century style.

The village of Pitmedden grew up around the crossroads of the Aberdeen–Tarves road and the road which leads to Oldmeldrum. It lies a little way east of Pitmedden House and garden, and had at its centre the church – originally the United Free Church for the area, which also housed the Free Church school. The oldest parts of the present school building date from 1874. Sir William Coote Seton, a supporter of the Free Church, granted a site in the village for a new church to be built in 1843. In January 1844, the first minister, the Rev. George Archibald, was ordained. Unfortunately the site of that church proved rather unsuitable, and the hall space which was used as a school below the church proper was prone to flooding. In 1864 William Coote Seton laid the foundation stone of the new church, built on higher ground on the opposite side of the road from the original one. The church's second minister, the Rev. George Abel, was something of a poet and produced a collection of works entitled *Wylins Fae My Wallet*, published in 1916. His poems were written in Doric, the dialect spoken in the north-east of Scotland, and were on a variety of topics, ranging from 'The Dominie' (schoolmaster) to 'Somewhere in France', a poem about a mother worrying about her soldier son, and including some poems on biblical topics. Pitmedden Church was united with Udny Green Church in 1931.

Tolquhon Castle. Tolquhon estate was created from one half of the lands of Sir Henry Preston of Fyvie, whose property was divided between his two daughters when he died. Marjory Preston, married to Sir John Forbes, inherited Tolquhon. The family built an impressive tower on the hill overlooking the countryside towards Tarves in the north and Pitmedden in the south in the early part of the fifteenth century. The tower formed the main residence of the Forbes family until 1582, when the 7th Laird, William Forbes, undertook an ambitious five-year building programme. When completed, the grand new building, constructed round a rectangular cobbled courtyard, boasted its own bakehouse, brewery and pit prison. The master mason, Thomas Leiper, also worked on Udny's Christ's Kirk and the mansion house at Schivas. In 1589 King James VI visited Tolquhon to admire the many splendours of the new building as a guest of the laird and his wife. The Forbes family's fortune declined over the following century, one laird sinking considerable funds into the ill-fated Darien Scheme. In 1716, the Forbes family of Tolquhon was forced to sell the estate to Lieutenant Colonel Francis Farquhar. William Gordon, Earl of Aberdeen, acquired the property less than 30 years later and it remained in the hands of the Gordons until 1929. By this time, the house was in a serious state of decay and the ruins were transferred to state care, and finally to Historic Scotland, which maintains the property to this day.

At the time of the Reformation, it was decreed that every kirk should have a school, and thus the parish school at Tarves came into being, the first records dating from 1611. In those days fees were 10 shillings per annum for day pupils and 16 shillings for boarders. There was no schoolhouse; the schoolmaster had to sleep in the church loft. In 1837 a new school and schoolhouse, shown here, were built to replace the stone, lime and turf school building of more than a century before. This new school was built on the north side of the Square with money from the Dick Bequest Educational Endowment. Latin, Greek and Mathematics were taught when required, as well as the traditional reading, writing and arithmetic. In 1896 a diphtheria epidemic saw school attendance drop by two-thirds. The school was eventually closed in February that year until the disease was under control. Fortunately, no school pupil died, and drainage and sanitary arrangements in the village were improved to prevent something like this happening again. After this school closed in 1911, the building was used for a variety of purposes, including a shoe factory and an electrician's workshop. It is now home to the Tarves Heritage Centre. George Melvin, considered an 'eccentric genius' because of his unorthodox teaching methods, was schoolmaster in Tarves in 1848. The village hall, which was built with the £400 he left to be used 'for some public purpose', is a lasting memorial to him.

The new school on the south side of Duthie Road was opened in 1911. Once a junior secondary, it is now a primary school and one of only two remaining schools in the parish, the other being in Barthol Chapel. Made from New Pitsligo granite, the school cost a little over £3,000 to build. An attendance officer, known as 'the Whipper In' was appointed to ensure the pupils attended regularly. No Latin or French was taught here, and those who wished to continue their education would travel to Methlick or Oldmeldrum, which had Higher Grade Schools, or to the Academy in Inverurie. With an emphasis on practical subjects at Tarves School, the School Board also took the circumstances of the Great War into account, granting exemptions for boys of thirteen who had to take their fathers' and older brothers' places on the family farms. One schoolteacher of around that era was Miss Margaret Noble, daughter of the gamekeeper of Udny Castle. She left her post in 1922 to marry Nathaniel Duncan, a war veteran, and son of the big house at Tillycorthie.

In the 1830s, Craigdam School was one of four in the parish, the others being in Tarves itself, at Auchedly and at Barthol Chapel. Craigdam School was built with a £600 bequest from a Mr Barron. Like many other rural schools, it closed in the early part of the twentieth century when fewer workers were required on the land, and people therefore started to find work in towns and cities and move away from their rural roots.

These houses are on the left of the road which leads in to Tarves from Aberdeen. In the foreground is the impressive home of Duthie Webster, heir to the Collynie Shorthorn herd. In the background is the building that was originally the girls' school in Tarves, from 1875 to 1883. Afterwards it was used as a cottage hospital until the early twentieth century. At the front were the nurses' quarters and behind that was the hospital wing. A plaque on the south wall remembers Mary Jane Greenhaugh, nurse at the Cottage Hospital until 1890.

The Square in Tarves, the east side of which is seen here, has barely changed in many respects, the facades of the original buildings remaining intact, although their purposes may have changed over the years. On the north side of the Square is the old school; Melvin Hall (not seen in this picture) is situated where the Square runs into Duthie Road. Once the Square and its adjoining streets boasted an old inn, a tailor and outfitters, the post office telegraph office, a chemist, a dressmaker, the Aberdeen Town and County Bank, a bakery, a saddler, a blacksmith, a joiner, another tailor, a watchmaker and three shoemakers.

To the south-east of the Square is Kirk Brae, the road here seen leading off on the left, a row of single-storey houses which is the oldest part of Tarves, and continues to look much as it did when the houses were first built. Across from the houses is the church. On that site there has been a church since approximately 600 AD when St Murdebur of Leinster brought Christianity to Tarves. The ancient church stood until 1798 when it was replaced with the present building. On the south side of the Square is the Aberdeen Arms Hotel (seen on the right of this picture), which has served the community for many years. Run by Duncan Rennie in the early part of the twentieth century, it was apparently only licensed to sell beer. Rennie also ran the local car hire business, hiring his car to Tarves people so that they could enjoy day trips. An older ale house on the old Aberdeen road was used as the trading centre for the stockings knitted by locals, which generated much-needed extra income and were sold far and wide.

To the west of the Square is Tarves's only remaining general store (seen in the distance on the right), run by the Duthie family. Initially, the Duthies ran a shop on the south side of the Square (the building in the centre of this view), where McHattie had run a tailor's business, before moving into the shop and post office premises across the Square. To the south of the Square there was once an almshouse, the Bede House, which was founded and endowed by William Forbes, the 6th Laird of Tolquhon, in the sixteenth century. In return for food, clothing, pay and lodgings, the poor men from Bede House had to attend their laird on Sundays and pray for the founder's soul. By 1735, the Forbes family was no longer at Tolquhon and the almshouse fell into ruins. Today, a street called Bede Way reminds us of the path taken by the men from Bede House to the Church.

Tree Road leads uphill from the north side of the Square. One of the large houses on its right-hand side was originally the local doctor's house and surgery. On the right side of the road, a row of small semi-detached cottages were built in the 1920s, each one being given the name of a tree.

The village of Tarves, looking east along Duthie Road. Duthie Road in Tarves was named after the village's most prestigious family. The road leads from the Square out of the village in a westerly direction to a crossroads which takes you to Cairnbrogie in one direction, Craigdam in another, and past Tillyhilt towards Keithfield and Methlick in a northerly direction.

The manse sits to the south of the church and the graveyard. One young resident of the manse in the 1930s, Miss Jean Murray, remembers being chased out of the churchyard for playing 'bools' – marbles – with her friends. She had strong Tarves connections: as well as being the minister's daughter, she was granddaughter of one of Tarves's headmasters, Alexander Pirie.

In the northern part of the parish of Tarves is the area known as Schivas. Schivas was a barony and having once been annexed to Methlick, was returned to Tarves parish in 1610. In those dim and distant days, several members of the Schivas family held positions of power in public life, notably Andrew de Syves, who was rector of Aberdeen Grammar School in the early fifteenth century, and William Schevez, who became Archbishop of St Andrews after an illustrious medical career as physician to Henry III. It is said that he practised the Black Arts in addition to normal medicine, astrology and theology. The Gray family then inherited Schivas, and built the ancestral home in the sixteenth century. It is this family that is responsible for the benign ghost said to haunt the house. In the seventeenth century, eighteen-year-old Mary Gray fell in love with a kinsman named John Leslie. Her father wanted her to marry someone else – a much older and wealthier man – and imprisoned his daughter in her home to stop her seeing her young lover. However, Leslie helped Mary to escape and they eloped. When Mary finally returned to Schivas, her father was dead. It is said that on the anniversary of her return to Schivas, the ghost of a happy girl can be seen crossing the paved courtyard, through the heavy castle door, up a spiral staircase and into her childhood chamber. Schivas estate has changed hands many times over the centuries, passing to the Forbeses of Craigievar in 1703, the Laird of Drum in the nineteenth century, and then to the 'Premier Earl', Lord Aberdeen of Haddo, in 1844. In 1900, a fire destroyed much of the building. It was subsequently rebuilt and extended.

The Howff is the burial enclosure of the Forbes family, who lived at Schivas from 1703 until the nineteenth century. The Howff is engraved with the initials H. F. and C. G., standing for Hugh Forbes and his wife, Christian Garden. During the terrible winter of 1782–3, when the harvest was ruined by early frosts and snow, Hugh Forbes and his wife put their tenants to work in clearing stones and boulders from the fields. By paying them a wage for their work, they ensured that their tenants would not starve.

Haddo House was built in the early eighteenth century in the Palladian style to replace the ruins of a big house at the Place of Kelly, destroyed by the Covenanters nearly a century before. The new house, designed by William Adam, was built by William Gordon, 2nd Earl of Aberdeen and constructed with the finest mortar and stone money could buy. The Gordon family can trace their roots at Haddo back over 500 years. In 1497, the first reference to the lands of 'Haldauch' (Haddo) appears in the record books; they were conveyed to James Gordon, who married Canea Harper, the heiress of the 'sunny half' of Methlick, and he later added the 'shadow half' of Methlick and other lands to his estate. The Gordons continued to add to their property, and gradually the whole Barony of Kelly, once owned by Robert the Bruce's great adversary, Alexander Comyn, Earl of Buchan, became theirs. Members of the Gordon family have been influential in many spheres of life, and their number includes a Bishop of Aberdeen, Alexander Gordon, who was appointed to that role in 1515. In the 1680s, the 1st Earl, Sir George Gordon, was appointed President of the Court of Session and Chancellor of Scotland. He played an influential role in the Treaty of Union in 1707. In addition to commissioning William Adam to design Haddo House, the 2nd Earl, William, added to his family's estate quite considerably, acquiring land at Tolquhon, Fyvie and other estates. His successor, the 3rd Earl, George, was something of the 'black sheep' of the family, famous for his womanising and self-indulgence.

Left: In every field, from the ministry to the army, the Gordons have achieved great success. In 1916, John, the 7th Earl, became Marquis of Aberdeen and Tremair. His successor, the 2nd Marquis, was prudent and careful, and in a time when many old families struggled to maintain their estates, he sold off 45,000 acres. The Deer Park Avenue of Haddo House is shown here. The house and its grounds are now safely in the hands of the National Trust for Scotland, and are open for all to enjoy. A theatre building near the big house is used as a centre for the arts. The Gordon family connection still remains, with June, Marchioness of Aberdeen, continuing to live in a wing of the house.

Left: The 4th Earl, George, was a prominent and well-respected figure of the nineteenth century. After losing a brother at the Battle of Waterloo, he helped to negotiate the peace with Napoleon at Amiens, and went on to have an illustrious career in politics, serving as Prime Minister of Great Britain from 1852 to 1855. Known as the 'Premier Earl', he was responsible for projecting Great Britain into the Crimean War, an act he seems to have deeply regretted. He also had a cultural side to him, being fascinated by Greek culture, an interest which earned him the nickname of the 'Athenian Aberdeen'. After his death, his grateful tenants erected the Prop of Ythsie as a memorial to him. This tall tower, positioned on a hill some miles from Haddo, can be seen from far and wide.

One unusual feature of the grounds at Haddo is the row of tiny gravestones which lines the avenue leading to the front of the house. The gravestones mark the last resting-places of the Gordon family's pet dogs from the past century. These touching reminders of faithful friends are tucked away under the mature trees. At the other end of the avenue is the obelisk erected in memory of the Premier Earl's brother, Sir Alexander Gordon, who fought with Wellington and was killed at Waterloo. A similar obelisk marks the scene of his death.

The River Ythan, which runs 30 miles from Wells of Ythan to the North Sea at Newburgh, has always been well stocked with fish but was once also rich with pearl oysters. Close to Haddo where the Kelly Burn runs into the Ythan, it is said that Sir Thomas Menzies of Cults found a large pearl which he presented to King James VI, in 1620. This pearl was incorporated into the Scottish crown. The Scottish crown jewels are now displayed in Edinburgh Castle.

Up until the 1930s, Methlick consisted of a single row of buildings along one bank of the River Ythan. The land of the parish, once all belonging to the Gordons of Haddo, was of mixed quality, much of it boggy. Nevertheless, the parish has always had farming at its heart, and in the nineteenth century there were well-attended cattle and horse markets, as well as so-called feein' markets, where local agricultural workers would go to seek their next six months' employment. The area supplied thousands of young, lean cattle each year for the calf dealers, who would drive the cattle to the south of Scotland and England for fattening and finishing. In ancient history, it is believed that Methlick was on the border between two hostile rural tribes, given the proliferation of flint arrowheads, burial mounds and cairns that have been found in the parish. It is also known that Roman troops were stationed at Ythan Wells, and that in their wake, following the course of the river, came St Ninian, who brought Christianity and the first chapel to the people of Methlick. There are no remains to be found of the first chapel at Andet, to the south of the village, but the site of St Devenick's well is noted on maps, to the north of the village, and people used to believe the waters could cure all ills. St Devenick's Feast Day, 13 November, was at one time celebrated in Methlick with a popular fair. The shop on the right of this picture is the general merchant's, once owned by the Grant family, and is still a family-run business.

The village of Methlick once supported bakers, butchers, two banks and two general stores. In addition, the Ythan View Hotel (seen here at the far left) was once known as the Institution, the scene of the Reading Club, founded in 1908 by the Rev. Mackenzie. Nowadays, Methlick has only one general store, which has been run by the same family for many years. One of Methlick's most famous sons was Dr Charles Maitland, originally of Auchincrieve. He was the man who introduced vaccination to Scotland and can thus be credited with saving many lives.

These scenes of Methlick from the east show the school, high above the village, and the site of the ruins of the former church and churchyard. Evidence suggests that there has been a church in Methlick since 1275. The church glebe was gifted to the parish in 1365. The former church's walls remain in the centre of this old churchyard. In it are the graves of various Gordons of Haddo, the last one to be buried there George, 5th Earl of Aberdeen, who died in 1864. The churchyard was used as a common meeting place for the parishioners waiting for the second bell to be admitted into the church on a Sunday morning, while nearby, the alehouses at Coblestakes were kept busy. In the eighteenth century, an elder was given the responsibility for checking the inns in Methlick, to catch parishioners who were drinking when they should have been attending the church service. In August, Methlick Church dispensed the sacrament of Holy Communion. Its preparation and thanksgiving occupied several days, and the congregation was expected to attend all of the services: on the Fast Day, Thursday; on the Day of Preparation, Saturday; two on the Sunday; and the Thanksgiving Service on Monday. Working on the Fast Day was considered sacrilegious, but in 1684 the parishioners of Balnagoak, Little Ardo, Hillbrae, Chapleton and Milton of Kelly were called before the Kirk Session and sharply rebuked for 'yoaking (working) on ye day of ye fast'.

Methlick

The present church in Methlick was built in 1866, across the burn from the earlier church and the graveyard. It was one of two in Methlick at that time, the second – the Free Kirk, built in 1848 – being situated at the top of the hill at the opposite side of the Ythan. Initially Free Church services in Methlick were held on grass fields north and south of the River Ythan, before a congregation of between 200 and 300 people. William Grant, a local merchant, rented his hall to them for a time until a site was found for the church and it was built. This building was eventually sold in 1939 after the union between the Free Church and the Church of Scotland. The church building (*above*) is regarded as one of the 'finest specimens of Presbyterian architecture in the country'. The building work was started by the 5th Earl of Aberdeen and completed after his death by his son. It was designed by architects Brown and Wardrop of Edinburgh, who made provision in the building for an organ, and in 1877 the parishioners petitioned Lord Aberdeen to have one installed. The clock tower was added in 1907 as a memorial to the Rev. Dr. J. Whyte, minister of the parish for 42 years.

The bridge over the Ythan, recently widened and strengthened, dates from 1844, when it was built to a design by John and William Smith. Before that, people crossed the Ythan from the eastern part of the parish by stepping stone or by ferry. Once, when the river was in spate, the weekly church service was cut short, to allow worshippers to make their way home safely. Along the road towards Ellon, there is another bridge which crosses the Ythan, at Tangland. This bridge was built in 1864 at the site of an earlier ford, which had been used as a crossing on the old drove road from Buchan to the south.

The War Memorial at Methlick was erected in 1921, paid for by public subscription. Fifty-one men from Methlick died in the First World War and they are also commemorated on a brass plaque inside the church, for which one of them, Captain George A. C. Moir, had left money in his will. When it was unveiled, the church was filled as the people of Methlick remembered their dead.

Reports of formal education in Methlick parish date from 1688. The school was under the control of the Church, as all schools were at that time. In 1690 a tragedy befell the scholars, when three boys were killed and the schoolmaster was severely injured during a thunderstorm. The present school, dating from 1913, replaced a school building first used in the 1830s. In the mid-nineteenth century, the schoolmaster at Methlick could expect to earn a princely £116 per annum. He also had the use of the schoolhouse, a building on the main street next situated next to the Institute, now the Ythan View Hotel. In 1846 a girls' school was opened, endowed by James Barrack of Inverebrie, who left £150 for the purpose. The building is now a private house known as Ivy Cottage. The girls studied reading, writing, arithmetic, geography, Scripture, history and needlework, the Bible was read daily, and the teacher had to be a member of the Church of Scotland. The trustees included the Earl of Aberdeen, the Minister and the Kirk Session. Financial assistance was given to those who could not pay the fees. In 1881 the School Board combined the boys' and girls' schools, Mr Alexander Keith being appointed as the first headmaster of Methlick Public School. In the nineteenth century there were also several rural schools, at Cairnorrie, Inverebrie, Throopmuir and Quilquox. Over the years, these rural schools have all been closed down.

On the border of Udny and Newmachar parishes, Whiterashes consists of a row of houses on either side of the main Aberdeen–Banff road. In the mid-nineteenth century, with an Episcopal Church, a hall, a school (pictured here) and a post office and shop, the tiny hamlet was at the centre of its farming community. It is no surprise that it hosted the first ever Formartine Agricultural Association meeting in 1829, and was the setting for the Association's annual show that year, and between 1834 and 1838.

Whiterashes is here seen from the south. A hall, built in 1922, is still in use, as is All Saints Episcopal Church, seen here on the right-hand side of the road, built in 1862, under the United Diocese of Aberdeen and Orkney. The estate of Pittrichie, comprising the farms of Coullie, Cairnfechel, Affleck, Auchinhuive and others was owned in the nineteenth century by two brothers, George and the Rev. John Robb, who was minister at Longside. The Robb family built an earlier hall at Whiterashes, to be used for Presbyterian worship, and in addition, John Robb left funds in his will to establish three bursaries, to enable children of the parishes of Udny, Longside and St Machar to enter higher education. These bursaries are still awarded annually to students.

The shop and post office at Whiterashes and the small school are all now closed. With Newmachar and Oldmeldrum a mere five minutes' drive away, Whiterashes simply does not need the facilities it once provided for the area.

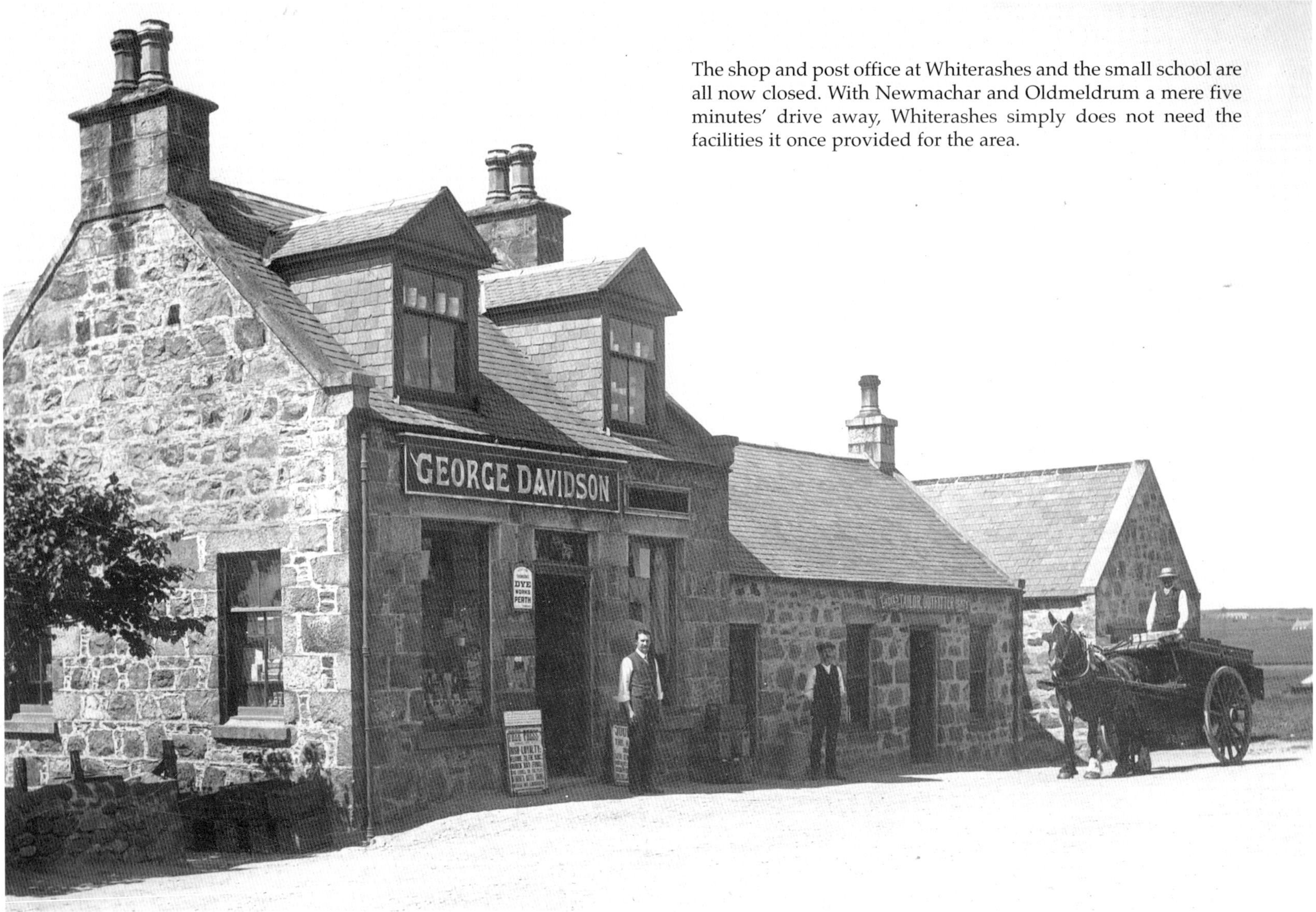